IT'S A HIT!

Written by Sharon Wohl
Illustrated by Dori Beeler

Creator of The Phonics Game™

Printed in the U.S.A.

A Better Way of Learning • www.phonicsgame.com

The sun is hot.
The fans get snacks.
The fans sit.

Jeff will pitch.
Jeff's cap is black.
Jeff grabs his cap.

Chet has a bat.
Chet swings.
Is it a hit?
Not yet.

Chet hits.
Chet runs and runs.
Chet is fast.

Can Beth catch the hit?
Yes!
The fans clap and yell.

Dan is up.
Jeff will pitch.
Thud, Dan's shin
gets hit.
The fans get mad.
Dan limps.

The kids switch.
Jen will pitch.
Jen's cap is red.
Ted is up. Can Ted hit?
Ted has 3 swings.
Ted sits back on the bench.

Sam is up.
Can Sam hit?
Wham, Sam hits.

The hit is up and up.
When will it stop?

Rex jumps.
Rex has Sam's hit.
Sam has a run!

Beth is up.
Beth hits and runs quick,
but Chet tags Beth.

Jeff's pal Wes is up.
Whack, this is the
best hit yet.

Wes runs and runs.
Wes runs past the ump.
Wes is in!

The fans jump up.
The fans clap.
The fans yell.

Beth, Ted, Wes, Jeff and
Sam hug.
It is fun to win!